Forward - First in a series of books for anyone, but aimed
be every day, true stories of Samson Parker who just happens to be a Rottweiler. We hope it
will educate people and let them know that the Rottweiler is a loyal, amazing dog who when
raised with the right family, is the best dog anyone could hope to have.

This book is dedicated to my father Robert, who has since passed away. Growing up, he
taught us that nothing can stand in your way if you want it bad enough and are willing to work
hard for it. He dedicated himself to a lifetime of taking care of his family, even though the
hardships he encountered would break any other person.

Hope in Their Hearts

This story begins at a home in New Jersey. This house was normally a very happy place. It was the home of the Parker family. The family consisted of a mom and dad and five kids aged five all the way to twenty. But today was a very sad day for the Parkers. Their beloved dog, Kali, had just died, and they could not imagine life without a dog.

It is said that when a dog dies, its spirit goes over the Rainbow Bridge. The bridge leads to all the other dogs that have died and passed over the bridge. It is also said that the doggies there are happy and play together forever.

As much as the Parkers tried to imagine Kali going over the Rainbow Bridge and having fun, they still felt the sadness of missing her. She would no longer be romping around the house and cuddling them all the time. What would their car trips be like without her riding with them, begging to stick her head out the window, and sitting in their laps? What would nighttime in the house be like without Kali faithfully patrolling the hallways, watching out for anything or anyone that would hurt them?

They all had so many questions running through their minds, but the biggest question of all was one everyone wanted to know. Would the Parkers get another dog? This one question brought a series of new questions. Would they love that new dog as much as Kali? Would their new dog love them as much as Kali did? When would they get one? They sat around the living room, crying and looking at Kali's toys, food bowls, and leash, and they knew they must have another dog.

One day, a few weeks after Kali went over the bridge, the Parker kids woke up to some big news from Mom and Dad. The entire family was to get dressed and clean up the house and get ready for a long car ride. Mom and Dad announced they were on their way to get a new puppy because they missed Kali so much. The kids shrieked with excitement so loudly that Mom and Dad covered their ears. They all knew a new dog could never replace Kali, but they would all enjoy raising another puppy.

They would have to take a long, long drive to a farm that sold puppies. Their friend Bob owned the farm, and he only raised one special breed of dog there: Rottweilers. Kali had been a Rottweiler, and the Parkers had always had a Rottweiler in their house. They had never owned another kind of dog, so all the Parker kids were raised with them. Rottweilers start out as tiny puppies but grow into huge, lovable, and loyal friends. Once the Parkers had a Rottie in their life, they never wanted to know life without one. All the Parkers liked big dogs, even though having one is not always easy.

Big dogs can step on your feet, get in your way, and bark as loud as thunder. Still, the Parkers had loved Kali so much that all of her big-dog behavior just made them love her more. They were excited and happy knowing they might come home with a new baby Rottweiler to complete their family once again.

They all got into the car and drove and drove and drove, chatting all the way there with hope in their hearts that they would find just the right pup. The car ride was so noisy and filled with excitement that Dad nearly missed the turn into the farm.

The Big Decision

When they arrived, Bob was outside waving at them. He took them into a big red barn.

Inside it was clean and smelled like hay, and the roof was so high that they could barely see where it stopped above. Bob took them to a little fenced area that had three puppies in it.

"These pups are twelve weeks old and ready to go to a new family," Bob explained. "There are two boys and one girl. Let's take them outside and see what you think!" Bob led the puppies out into the yard so that everyone could meet them. They were stumbling around because they were new babies and were still clumsy on their feet. Those little puppies followed Bob right out the door.

The Parkers couldn't help grinning at each other as they followed Bob and the pups outside to the yard. The sun was shining brightly, and there was loads of room for the puppies to run. They were like three little clowns, playing with each other, chasing each other, and falling into somersaults on the lush green grass. The puppies looked exactly alike with their soft black fur shining in the sun. Their faces were so cute with their little light-brown eyebrows like half-moons above their big brown eyes. They were all so lovable—how would the Parkers choose?

As they watched, they noticed that two of the puppies seemed to hang around each other all the time.

The third puppy, meanwhile, insisted on sniffing all the Parkers and was not shy toward them. He was trying hard to get noticed—he kept running from one Parker to the next and wagging his little stump of a tail the entire time. One by one, the Parkers fell in love as they interacted with him, and he was not afraid of them. When they moved, he followed. When they cuddled him, he licked. One of the kids said, "I think he wants to come home with us!"

When the puppy heard these words out loud, he started jumping and running from kid to kid. His heart was beating fast in his little chest. He was so happy that the family seemed to know what he was thinking. He was trying his best to let them know he had made his mind up. He wanted to be a Parker.

"This is a big choice to make," Dad said. "Is this the puppy you want to take home?"

All at once, all the kids were nodding and yelling, "Yes, yes, he is the one!" That was the moment the Parkers got their newest family member.

The First Car Ride

The Parkers scooped him up and took turns holding him. He went first to his new sister Linzee, the oldest Parker child. Then to Taylor, the youngest. This puppy seemed big to Taylor, but she was only five years old, so he was big to her. She had a hard time holding him on her own because he was squirming and wriggling in her arms. She felt her arms and legs getting scratched. Taylor cried, and Mom and Dad asked her to put the puppy down. They said it would be better if she sat down and held him in her lap. That was a funny sight to see. He seemed so big in her arms.

Bob took the pup away for just a few minutes. He put him up on a high table, and the Parkers surrounded him while Bob gave him a nail clipping and a hair brushing and took his picture. He looked so handsome, and he felt wonderful.

Then the Parkers took their new family member into their minivan and started the long journey home.

Once again, Taylor wanted to hold the puppy. Mom and Dad explained that it would not be safe

for him. In addition, they reminded her of the scratches she received once the puppy got nervous.

Then they decided to let Taylor see for herself. They strapped Taylor into her car seat and

promptly handed the puppy to her. That did not work out too well, and poor Taylor finally

understood that she and the pup would be much safer if he were in the back with the bigger kids.

They decided to settle him into the car next to Linzee. Being the oldest, and sitting in the biggest

seat, she could make the ride home a better experience for all.

While Dad was driving, the new pup moved closer to Linzee so she could comfort him. He kept wiggling closer and closer and appeared nervous. Just then, Linzee shouted, "Mom, the puppy is gagging. I think he is going to throw up!" Dad was on a highway and could not pull the car over.

All the kids started screaming and crying. "Is he going to be okay?"

Mom was calm. She had seen this many times before. She told all the kids that they needed to quiet down so they did not scare the puppy. She handed Linzee some paper towels, and as soon as Linzee got them in her hands, the puppy started to throw up.

Mom said, "He will be fine. He is just not used to being in a car. He will feel better when he is done throwing up."

Linzee remembered this exact situation when they brought Kali home. She said to the kids, "Mom is right. He will be fine, and he will love riding in the car once he gets used to it, just like Kali did."

Shortly, the puppy felt better. His little tummy was still not feeling normal, but he felt happy. He knew that everyone in the car was concerned about him, and that felt good. He looked up at his new sister with love because she had helped and comforted him. He was fine the rest of the way home and did not get sick again. Dad drove, and everyone in the car tried to be a bit quieter so they didn't scare the new puppy. The ride seemed quick, and soon they pulled up in front of their house.

When the puppy first walked in the door, there was just one step going down into the living room. It seemed gigantic to him, and he was afraid to go down. The kids went into the living room, and Mom and Dad stayed behind him, just before the step. He cautiously stepped down with one paw, but his stubby little legs could not reach the floor, so he tumbled down the rest of the way.

Everyone ran to help him, but after his somersault, he was happily lying in the middle of the floor with every Parker around him, petting him, soothing him, and smiling at him.

Let the Names Begin

During their bonding time, Mom and Dad mentioned that the puppy would need a name. Once again, the noise level rose very high in the house. Everyone started shouting out names and trying to talk loudly so their choices could be heard. The puppy ran away thinking that everyone was angry with him. Mom reminded the kids that this puppy was new and that he had grown up on a quiet farm. She said that his only contact with humans was when Bob and his family would come into the barn to take care of the dogs. Mom sternly told them to stop shouting.

Dad mentioned that everyone would have to agree on one name. He came up with a plan. He went into his office and came back with pieces of paper and a handful of pens. He passed the paper pieces out to each person, along with a pen. He instructed them to write their favorite puppy names on the paper pieces and fold them up really small in order to keep them secret. He then took off his baseball cap and asked the family to put their papers into the hat. He had Mom close her eyes and pick one of those papers out. He said that whatever name she drew, that would be the name of the dog. He asked if everyone agreed. There was still some whining and grumbling, but in the end, they all agreed.

They finished writing their names and folded their papers up small, just like Dad had asked them to do. Mom closed her eyes, and Dad guided her hand to the cap to pick out just one name. Each kid held his or her breath, and she handed the paper to Dad, who would read out the name.

"Samson," he said. "Samson Parker will be the puppy's name." At first the room was very quiet. The kids were trying to absorb this new information. Then, like magic, everyone was happy and agreed that "Samson" was the perfect name for the new puppy. As it turned out, "Samson" was the name that Mom had written down. She was pretty good at naming, as it turned out.

Right away, everyone started calling him by his new name and every version of that name as well. He got some new nicknames. The family called him Sam, Sammy, Samsonite, and other names that came from "Samson." As long as they were fussing over him, he did not care what they called him.

The family took Sam into the kitchen to show him where he would be eating. They had purchased two matching white bowls with colorful little paw prints on them. One bowl was for food, and one was for water. Samson ate and drank right away, which showed that he felt right at home.

Throughout the day, they took him outside to his new yard and continued to pet him, cuddle him,

play with him, and give him all their love. Samson had never known this type of love. His dog mom had cared for him, and Bob and the workers at the farm had petted him from time to time. Still, the affection from his new family was better than anything he could imagine. He absolutely loved it. He was so excited, but he also felt tired after his big day. His little eyes kept drooping, and the Parkers noticed it was time for bed. They took him out in the back for one last bathroom trip and then scooped him up to show him his new sleeping place.

That night, his new mom and dad took Sammy to their room. The plan was to have Samson sleep on the floor so he could be walked by his new mommy first thing in the morning. Poor Sammy just could not sleep without the comfort of his brother and sister. He cried loudly next to the bed, and it broke the Parkers' hearts. Within minutes, Sammy was lifted onto Mom and Dad's bed and nestled into the soft pillows between them. Samson was in heaven. He felt like a king sitting on a throne of pillows.

Over the next few months, Sammy would sleep here every single night, as happy as could be. But it wasn't long before he couldn't fit on the king pillows. His legs grew long, and his feet were kicking Mom and Dad in the head at night. It was time to have Sammy sleep on the carpet next to the bed. The parents also left their bedroom door open so that Sam could wander freely about the house at night. He would soon learn to "patrol" the house, taking turns sleeping in front of each bedroom and watching over all the Parkers as they slept.

Samson Meets the Neighborhood

Samson's new neighborhood was filled with nice people and loads of children. Samson was introduced to everyone, and he loved them all immediately. The neighborhood animals mostly loved him too, except the cats, who kept their distance and hissed a bit when he tried to lick them. He made many new friends in his little cul-de-sac, including his first friend Cassie, a small black-and-white dog. When they first met, she and Sam were the same size, but little by little, Samson grew and grew, and soon he was much bigger than Cassie.

Cassie and Sam were great friends. They enjoyed seeing each other every morning at the school-bus stop while they waited for the children to hop onto the bus and go to school.

Sammy loved all his dog friends. That included Rocky, Flash, Mimi, Chase, Bagel, and Cody. He loved playing outside with his buddies. They all shared toys and running around until they were exhausted. They were also happy to go home.

Sam's best friend of all was a very special dog named Maya. She did not live in the neighborhood, but Maya's parents were best friends with the Parkers, so they come over quite often. They never missed a birthday or holiday. When Maya came, she and Sammy got to spend hours together while their humans were catching up. They liked to lie on the floor, eat, and go on walks. Sometimes they even got to have overnight visits, when the families stayed together. They also enjoyed going out in the fenced-in yard by themselves. Sammy liked it when people walked by and saw him and Maya together. He was so proud to be her best friend. Maya lived in the country and did not see many dogs or cats. She was so thankful to have Samson as a best friend. And he felt exactly the same about her.

Not everyone in the neighborhood was a dog lover. As Samson grew and grew, people were afraid of him, and he just couldn't understand it. When people tried to walk or run away, he would try desperately to run after them. He just knew if he could give that first kiss to them that they would be friends for life.

It was hard for Samson to understand that some people just didn't like Rottweilers. He wondered why some humans would dislike him just because of the way he looked. Sammy could not help how he was born, after all. Some people thought he was mean just because he was so big and his fur was dark. Some people were not very nice to Sammy or his family when they walked outside of their friendly neighborhood. The Parkers taught all their children, including Samson, that some people just didn't like you no matter what you did. It should not matter how you look or how you were born. But your family was always there for you and would love you unconditionally.

The Parkers started daily routines of walking and training Sammy so that he would know how to act in public. Sam eventually learned to listen to his family when he was walking on his leash. If someone walked by who didn't like dogs, he stiffened his body, held his head straight, kept his eyes facing forward, and just walked by them. He knew that his family members would reward him by petting and hugging and kissing him, so it all turned out fine in the end.

Sammy's days were happy and filled with fun. He was looking forward to all his upcoming adventures with the Parkers.

FROM THE AUTHORS

We hope sincerely that you enjoyed your first Samson Parker book. Please check out our website in order to get more information about the Parkers, their dogs, and general information on Rottweilers: www.rottweilertales.com.

Samson Parker also has his own Facebook Page (Samson Parker).

ONCE A MONTH PRIZE GIVEAWAY:

www.rottweilertales.com/contest.html

Once a month, one lucky winner will be randomly selected to receive a Samson Parker plush toy (see picture below). Please click the contest link above and fill out the brief survey, and a plush Rottweiler could be on its way to you!

Please allow four to six weeks for delivery.

For each book purchased, one dollar will automatically be donate to the Northeast Rottweiler Rescue: http://www.rottrescue.org/

ROTTWEILER FACTS
For a full list of facts, please visit us at

http://www.rottweilertales.com/rottweilertales.html

 Never get any dog if it is not going to be a part of your family. People get Rottweilers in their homes and do not realize how large and boisterous they will get—and the solution too often is to put them outside. Rotties don't like to be on chains outside your homes, looking in, watching their humans having fun without them. Each moment you leave your Rottweiler, you break its heart. Remember that while you have a full life, they only have you.

 Owning a Rottweiler is a huge commitment. Because they are such a smart breed, they tend to take over in a family as "alpha" if not trained properly. You must commit to daily training for the lifetime of your Rottweiler. Puppies are loads of work with any breed, but Rotties are very smart and will try to be in charge whenever possible. You need to let this breed know who is boss.

 This breed needs to be exercised on a daily basis because they are lazy by nature and will enjoy just lying around and eating. The leaner you can keep your Rottie, the longer his life span will be. The exercise will be good for both of you. You should never approach a dog without asking the owner if it is okay to pet that dog. And you should never allow strangers to approach your dog unless you are there to hold the dog and assure him that everything is fine.

 Some people think that Rottweilers are nasty by nature, and as a result, Rotties get a bad reputation. Rottweilers are just like any animal. If you treat them kindly, they will respond with kindness. If you are mean to them, they will be forced to go on the defensive. Because a Rottie is a dog that will be over fifty pounds, they can do more damage than a smaller breed. Therefore, if your Rottweiler is not well trained, you have a potential weapon on your hands.

 Rottweilers are clowns and love to be the center of attention. They need love and playtime with their humans. While it is difficult to ignore the equivalent of a baby "horse" running around your house, sometimes people get mad when they get stepped on or pushed over. This responsibility is that of the human. It boils down to training. Don't allow your Rottweiler to jump. Don't play tug-of-war games with your Rottweiler. If you put your Rottie in a position where it can win or lose, it will most certainly want to win. People, especially small ones, can get hurt because this breed is so large.

Rottweilers love to push their rear ends into you and lean on you if they love you. They also tend to step on your feet. Please wear slippers or shoes in your house when playing with your Rottie.

Please visit us at:

www.rottweilertales.com

Keep up with the progress of all our books.

Made in the USA
Middletown, DE
20 January 2021